AF292295

Expert Secrets – CBT & Emotional Intelligence

The Ultimate Guide for Cognitive Behavioral Therapy & EQ to Improve Anger Management, Anxiety, Depression, Insomnia, Negative Thinking, Panic, and Stress!

Terry Lindberg

"Expert Secrets – CBT & Emotional Intelligence: The Ultimate Guide for Cognitive Behavioral Therapy & EQ to Improve Anger Management, Anxiety, Depression, Insomnia, Negative Thinking, Panic, and Stress!" Written by "Terry Lindberg".

Expert Secrets – CBT & Emotional Intelligence is a bundle of the books "Expert Secrets – Emotional Intelligence", & "Expert Secrets – Cognitive Behavioral Therapy (CBT)".

Hope You Enjoy!

Expert Secrets – Emotional Intelligence

The Ultimate Guide for EQ to Improve Anger Management, CBT, Empath, Manipulation, Persuasion, Self-Awareness, Self-Discipline, Self-Regulation, and Social Skills.

Terry Lindberg

Table of Contents

Chapter 6: Strategies for Improving Emotional Intelligence

1. Self-Awareness
2. Self-Regulation
3. Motivation
4. Empathy
5. Social skills

Hey, it's Terry Lindberg,

Before we start, I want to tell you about an exclusive offer just for readers of this book...

When starting your self-help journey, the one thing that you must have in check is your mindset. If your mindset is not up to scratch you are setting yourself up for failure before you have even started.

To have the mindset shift that you'll need to set you up for success; you have to do endless amounts of research to get mental clarity, acquire new daily habits, and much more.

Sounds like hard work, right?

Well yes, it would be, but luckily for you, I have partnered up with Intelligence Mastery. Who are giving away their highly rated course that will give you all of the step-by-step process for shifting your mindset into gear seamlessly!

Best thing about this exclusive offer is it 100% FREE, no-strings-attached. Intelligence Mastery usually charge $297 for this exact same course to their customers

All you need to do to claim your FREE the Ultimate Mindset Course; is in your search browsers URL go to – free.intelligencemastery.com

Once you are on the web page, fill out the required information that Intelligence Mastery asks for; this should only take less than 1 minute of your time. Then straight away in your email inbox you will receive the life changing course that has helped 10,000's of people around the world.

Before reading any further, please do this NOW as I may refer back to some of the units in the course throughout this book!

free.intelligencemastery.com

Who Is Terry Lindberg?

Hello, and Thank you for purchasing a copy from the "Expert Secrets – Self Help Series."

For all of you who do not know who I am, my name is Terry Lindberg, an award-winning Psychologist and Author of the Expert Secrets – Self Help Series. I have dedicated 30+ years of my entire life for innovating the field of psychology and self-help to improve mine and 1000's of other's lives across the globe ranging from top CEO's in their area to the best athletes, and even just regular individuals.

The one thing I can say about everyone who I have worked with is that they see dramatic changes in their lives following my teachings. My teachings help them to push through barriers they never thought they could get through. In most cases, the same outcome happens; they witness a switch go off in their mind, showing them the human brain is far more powerful than they could ever think was imaginable.

Throughout the entire 30+ years of my life studying in the field of psychology and self-help, I have acquired wisdom and unique experiences from the people who I have worked alongside and interviewed. The vast amount of knowledge that I have gained is everything that I will be passing onto you within this book.

This guide is not like any other self-help book out there, as to be honest 99% of self-help books on the market are not even made by someone within the field. They have partnered up with a ghost-writer to produce the contents of the book, then packaged and marketed to you as if it was made by someone who has experience in that topic.

The information that I will share with you has proof of concept and will actually assist you at whatever point you are on your journey.

Have you ever heard of the theory "The Golden Nugget" when reading a book? This theory means that an entire book could be irrelevant to the topic, but yet there could be one "Golden Nugget" of information that could be life-changing.

Because of this theory, I want you to be prepared and make sure for the the length of this entire book that I have your full attention. By the way, if you didn't notice that the sentence before said "the" back to back, you're not paying enough attention.

Drop everything you are doing, focus on in, and be prepared to take notes. You may be only one sentence away from changing your life forever.

If you learn or like anything about the content, you have consumed when finished. An honest review is always appreciated for helping me make better content in the future.

Now let's get started...

Introduction

Have you ever felt irrationally angry at something someone said or did? Do you experience emotional outbursts, and you just cannot pinpoint where they come from? Do you frequently find yourself manipulated by people? Luckily, you're not the only one. Understanding and dealing with emotions is a battle that countless individuals face on a daily basis. Problems with anger management, manipulation, empathy, and social skills are just some of the challenges that people face in their day-to-day lives. These problems are all intricately linked to a person's emotional intelligence. This book will provide you with an understanding of these challenges and where they originate, as well as a number of strategies that can be applied to addressing them. Through reading this book, you will see how these issues can be tackled through a deep understanding of emotional intelligence, its influence on the various sectors of human life, and how improving one's emotional intelligence can ease the process of dealing with these issues and others that may arise.

This book will equip you to deal with those unavoidable problems that emerge in your professional, personal, and social life. By studying the intricacies of emotional intelligence, you will gain a clearer understanding of the tremendous role that it plays in every aspect of your daily life. In this book, I will provide you with a number of strategies that will help you to improve your emotional intelligence, and subsequently help you in addressing problems with anger management, manipulation, empathy, social skills, and more. By improving your self-awareness, self-regulation, motivation, empathy and social skills, you will indefinitely improve your emotional intelligence.

My name is Terry Lindberg. I am an award-winning self-help author and psychologist. I have dedicated more than 30 years of my life to the advancement and innovation of the field of psychology and self-help in an effort to improve my life and thousands of other lives across the globe—ranging from top CEOs, to the best athletes, and even regular individuals. I want to show you that, with the help of the right person, you can improve your emotional intelligence significantly. In doing so, you will be equipped to become a better leader, partner, and friend.

By understanding the inner workings of emotional intelligence, you will be able to improve your emotional intelligence, function more effectively in the workplace, improve the quality of your relationships, and gain a better understanding of yourself. By gaining a better understanding of your emotions and the ability to identify them as they arise, you will be able to deal more constructively with the people around you. You will also experience a significant improvement in conflict resolution skills. Understanding emotional intelligence not only helps with understanding and dealing with your own emotions more effectively, but you will also be able to better identify and understand the emotions of other people. Emotional intelligence will directly impact your social, personal, and professional life. Raising your emotional intelligence level will equip you to be a better friend, co-worker, and a better person in general. There are countless benefits to understanding and improving your emotional intelligence, and these benefits will be thoroughly explored throughout the course of this book.

People spend unbelievably large amounts of money trying to learn how to manage their emotions through therapy sessions, meditation, anger-management classes, and yoga. This guide will teach you all you need to know about understanding and effectively managing your emotions. I will provide you with all the necessary information about the role of emotional intelligence in your life. You will learn how to understand yourself and others better, and consequently gain a better understanding of conflict resolution and relationships—both personal and professional. By simply understanding where their anger comes from and being more cognizant of their emotions, I have helped a number of people to overcome their anger management issues. By applying the strategies mentioned in this book, many people have learned to manage their emotions more effectively and are able to refrain from lashing out at others.

Through this guide, I will equip you to become an all-around success story. You will be able to address issues of anger management, manipulation, empathy, and social skills more effectively and efficiently. You will be able to build more meaningful personal and professional relationships and have a better understanding of yourself and others. You will be able to address conflict in a healthy and mature manner, both internally and externally. This guide will provide you with all you need to know about emotions and inform you on how to identify emotions more effectively and deal with them in a healthy way.

"When dealing with people, remember you are not dealing with creatures of logic, but with creatures of emotion" (Carnegie, n.d.). These words by Dale Carnegie could not be truer. Countless arguments and conflicts arise because people act and react out of emotion, rather than logic. Pride is one of the biggest causes of conflict in contemporary society, and very few people know how to deal with their emotions effectively. Once a person understands both their own emotions and the emotions of others, they are better equipped to identify them. Rather than suppressing these emotions, they are then able to deal with their emotions constructively and are able to manage the various aspects of their life more effectively. People with a high level of emotional intelligence are not subject to their emotions and understand that their emotions need not be the driving force behind their actions. Emotionally intelligent people act from a logical position, rather than reacting from an emotional disposition. There is no reason to struggle with uncontrollable emotions, unnecessary conflict or miscommunication mishaps any longer. This book will help you to overcome and avoid such situations efficiently and successfully.

The chapters in this book are formulated to take you through the process of understanding and mastering your emotions. Every chapter in this book explores a different aspect of emotional intelligence, and will eventually lead you to a number of strategies that will help you to improve your emotional intelligence, thus helping you to better understand your emotions and the emotions of others. Upon completing this book, you should be able to manage your emotions more effectively, create meaningful relationships and conduct yourself in a professional and confident manner. Improving your emotional intelligence will invariably increase your chances of leading a successful life.

Chapter 1: Understanding Emotions

Understanding your emotions and how emotions work is the first step to understanding and mastering emotional intelligence. By understanding your emotions, you will be able to understand yourself better and identify emotions more easily as they arise. Being aware of your emotions will help you to deal more effectively with them, instead of ignoring and suppressing your feelings.

In this chapter we will take a look at what emotions are, where they come from, and why we need them. Understanding these three questions will lay the groundwork for understanding emotional intelligence.

What Are Emotions?

Emotions are essentially a response to your surroundings and circumstances. This response occurs both psychologically and physiologically. Emotions can therefore be recognized both physically and mentally. There are three general stages in which an emotion takes place.

1. Physiological response

Emotions often provoke a physical response, or a change in one's physical state that occurs simultaneously with the emotion that is experienced. For instance, you may start sweating when you experience fear, or feel your stomach lurch when you feel anxious. These physiological changes occur unconsciously and can be helpful in identifying your emotions. Different people may experience different physiological reactions to the same emotion. So, it is important to get to know your own personal response.

2. Subjective experience

This stage involves the experience of the emotion itself. Each person experiences an emotion differently, and each person may describe the emotion uniquely. Emotions are therefore highly subjective experiences.

3. Behavioral response

During the behavioral response, the emotion is expressed and can be recognized by others. You may smile when experiencing happiness, for example, or frown as a result of confusion. These responses may be shaped by societal norms or individual experiences. If one person's parents frown when they are worried, for example, they will associate a frown with worry, whereas another person might associate it with anger or disgust based on their own history.

People's emotions are often determined and influenced by what, or who, they are surrounded by. Emotions are part of the human consciousness and communicate essential information about the core needs and desires a person might experience or require. Experiencing certain emotions can motivate us to either continue with our actions—in the case of pleasurable experiences—or to change our actions when we experience negative reactions or emotions. When a person dances with someone they love, for example, the experience would be pleasurable and they would therefore experience positive emotions. These positive emotions—happiness, love, or affection—convey the message that the person should continue the action. When speaking to someone who makes you feel uncomfortable, on the other hand, you might experience fear or disgust. These emotions communicate the need to walk away from the person or to go somewhere else. Emotions prepare people for action, thus the "fight or flight" analogy.

Emotions can be either positive or negative, and both positive and negative emotions should be acknowledged. When negative emotions are ignored or suppressed frequently, they have a negative effect on the person suppressing them. People who suppress their emotions rather than dealing with them, tend to erupt in a volcano-like fashion at a later stage. Their emotions often become intense and overwhelming, and they lose their ability to regulate their emotions effectively.

People have varying emotional temperaments, however. Some can manage negativity better than others, and some are more prone to experiencing, and reacting from, strong emotion. A person's emotional temperament will affect the intensity and regularity of certain emotions, and often affects a person's level of reaction to these emotions also. This can be remediated, however, by improving one's level of emotional intelligence.

Most people agree that there are six basic emotions. These are anger, fear, disgust, surprise, happiness, and sadness. All other emotions stem from these basic emotions. These emotions might not occur in their pure form. For instance, one might feel a mixture of surprise and fear or anger and disgust. Furthermore, the intensity and experience of the emotions differ based on the situation and the person experiencing the emotion. Instead of experiencing anger, for example, a person might experience blind rage. Emotions can be simple or complex, and some emotions may be harder to decipher than others. Emotions are also influenced by thought and perception, and shaped by experience.

Many people consider the concepts of emotions and moods to be synonymous. Although these concepts are very similar, they are not the same. Moods tend to last much longer than emotions and are often heightened and intensified by thought. Emotions, on the other hand, are feelings and momentary. We cannot control our emotions. We do, however, have a hand in controlling our moods.

Where Do Emotions Come From?

Emotions are common among all living species. The thing that sets human beings apart from other species, however, is that we are able to recognize our emotions and make judgements on the viability of these emotions. You might experience anxiety before an important test, for example. Your mind knows that the test is important and your thoughts are mustering up all the things that might happen, should you fail the test. You are able to recognize these feelings of anxiety, however, and declare them invalid. You know that you have studied for the test and your chances of failing the test are slim to none. We can think through and work through our emotions before we act, unlike other living species who feel and react impulsively.

Our emotions are based on our experiences. Our experiences help us form associations, which form part of our new experience of emotions. One person's associations with anticipation might be excitement, for example, because they are often pleased with surprises. You, on the other hand, might not experience anticipation quite as positively. Suppose that when you were nine years old, you were anticipating your birthday because you knew that birthdays were exciting and enjoyable. At the surprise party, however, you had a fright, fell down a flight of stairs and broke an arm and a leg. Since this incident, you associate anticipation with anxiety and fear, and possibly even pain. You dislike unpredictability because of your frame of reference for surprises.

Emotions can also be contagious. In the case of a funeral, for example, a person might become sad because of the grief that is displayed by those around him, rather than his own grief. The contagiousness of laughter is another example. It is important that we be aware of where our emotions come from to be able to decipher the message they are communicating to us more effectively.

Why Do We Need emotions?

Emotions are a central part of human consciousness. They are what motivate us to take action. Our actions are fueled by desire which, in turn, is fueled by our emotions. Emotions communicate important information to us about our desires and needs. We are then able to take these emotions and evaluate what it is that we want or need. Emotions are therefore central to our decision-making process. Our decisions are led by our emotions, based on our needs and desires. Experiencing loneliness, for example, signals the need for human connection. When one analyzes this emotion, they are able to determine that they are in need of a companion.

On a basic level, emotions are a survival instinct, meant to protect us from ourselves or from certain situations. When we experience a threat, we are able to react in order to preserve our safety. When we experience fear, for example, we know that there may be something in the vicinity that could jeopardize our sense of security. As a result of that fear, we are able to flee from the situation before the threat becomes imminent.

Emotions provoke certain physical and psychological responses that inform us of what we are feeling. When we feel nervous, for example, our palms may become sweaty. These physiological responses help us to identify our emotions so that we can assess our situation. There are certain psychological responses that also accommodate certain emotions, although these are harder to identify and much more complex.

Emotions not only protect us and inform us on a primitive level, however. Emotions also serve as social cues. When we are able to identify a person's emotions based on their body language or facial expression, we can determine a number of things. People's emotions can reflect their disposition toward you, in other words the nature of your relationship. It can also provide important information regarding the conversation. When a person is yawning, for example, it may indicate that they find the conversation boring or uninteresting. This emotional clue then provides you with a warning that you should change the direction of the conversation. Social cues help us to build better relationships and engage more effectively with others.

Without emotions, our lives would be primitive and dull. Emotions add depth to our lives and allow us to experience things like love, creativity, and inspiration. These things can make life richer and add value to our existence.

Chapter 2: Emotional Intelligence

Emotional intelligence, sometimes referred to as EQ, is the ability to identify and differentiate one's emotions as they arise. It involves being conscious of your emotions and being able to understand and effectively manage these emotions once they have been identified. Emotional intelligence helps guide you through your own thoughts, emotions, and behaviors, and helps you make sense of and understand them better. Emotionally intelligent people often make better and more responsible decisions, since they act logically and tend to think things through rather than reacting from their emotional disposition.

Not only does emotional intelligence help in the identification of your own emotions, behaviors, and thoughts, but it also helps with the identification and understanding of the emotions and behaviors of others. Emotional intelligence increases your capabilities of working well with people and understanding them more deeply. It will help you significantly in making sense of the behaviors and reactions of other people, since you will be better equipped to understand how they are feeling. When you understand what emotions are and where they come from, it is easier to sympathize with others and to manage emotionally charged situations.

Although intelligence, or IQ, is a useful tool, scientists agree that having a high level of intelligence is not enough. They argue that having a high EQ is equally important to succeed in life. In an age of globalization and social interaction, working with diverse people is an integral part of life as we know it. Emotional intelligence helps us to do this responsibly and effectively. Emotional intelligence is different from IQ in that it can be acquired and refined through practice.

There are five characteristics that are commonly linked with emotional intelligence. These characteristics are self-awareness, self-regulation, motivation, empathy, and social skills. Having a balance in these characteristics can prove very beneficial and can simplify the process of working with others.

1.   *Self-Awareness*

One of the characteristics of people who are emotionally intelligent is self-awareness. Self-awareness involves being conscious of your emotions and recognizing them as they occur. It involves understanding your emotions and tuning in to your feelings. Emotionally intelligent people do not avoid negative emotions. Rather, they identify these emotions and try to understand where they originated. Negative emotions should be processed rather than inhibited, since inhibiting negative emotions can be detrimental to both physical and mental health. Emotionally intelligent people are aware of this fact and are therefore able to work through their emotions more effectively. They take the time to reflect on and work through them rather than reacting immediately based on a feeling.

People with a high level of emotional intelligence usually know themselves well and are cognizant of their own strengths and weaknesses. Those who are self-aware have high levels of self-confidence and tend to be very conscious of their emotions, where their emotions come from, and how these emotions affect their thought patterns and behavior. Emotionally intelligent people understand that perfection is an unattainable standard. They are able to acknowledge their vulnerability and take responsibility for their mistakes and weaknesses.

2. *Self-Regulation*

Self-regulation is another aspect of emotional intelligence. This aspect involves a person's ability to control their emotions and impulses. People who have mastered self-regulation are able to refrain from making impulsive and careless decisions based on their feelings. Emotionally intelligent people don't allow their emotions to control their decision-making. They are often thoughtful and make thorough considerations instead of making impulsive or rash decisions based on their feelings. Those with high levels of emotional intelligence are skilled at self-control and practice conscientiousness.

Emotionally intelligent people are comfortable with change and are able to adapt to sudden changes more easily and effectively. They don't allow unpredictable changes to throw them off guard or affect their functioning. Instead, they acknowledge that change is inevitable and unavoidable, and therefore try to adapt with minimal disturbances. Mastering self-regulation also gives one the ability to say no when necessary, thus avoiding numerous uncomfortable situations. Emotionally intelligent people are usually much better at managing and controlling their emotions, moods, and reactions. They tend to live more balanced lives. They don't take on more responsibility than they can handle.

3. *Motivation*

Emotionally intelligent people often have clear and achievable goals. They are generally more productive and effective in what they do. They are open to new challenges and work hard to achieve that which they set out to accomplish. Emotionally intelligent people practice optimism and try to keep a positive attitude as much as possible. They don't allow temporary failures and setbacks to affect their long-term goals. They accept that failure is an integral part of life and should not be taken personally.

When emotionally intelligent people commit to something, they follow through on their commitment to the best of their abilities. They are driven and bent upon achieving success. Emotional intelligence improves self-discipline and will-power, thus making emotionally intelligent people significantly more productive in general. Emotionally intelligent people don't allow temporary failures to affect and derail their long-term goals. They acknowledge that failure is a part of the learning process and learn from their mistakes. They use their failures and mistakes to fuel their efforts.

4. *Empathy*

People with a high level of emotional intelligence tend to be very empathetic. Empathetic people are able to identify with and understand the needs of others. Emotional intelligence enables you to better recognize the emotions of others. Consequently, people who are emotionally intelligent are more competent at managing relationships and listening and relating to others. Emotionally intelligent people avoid stereotyping and jumping to conclusions at all cost. They are more prone to try and understand others' perspectives and are therefore able to understand and connect to others more easily. They tend to accept the views of others, regardless of whether they agree with these views. Emotionally intelligent people know that opposing views are not an attack on their perceptions, but merely a different way of seeing.

Emotionally intelligent people are not only considerate of the emotions of others, but they also anticipate how their actions and behaviors will affect themselves *and* other people. They consider others' needs along with their own and refrain from making decisions that will unnecessarily hurt others.

5. *Social Skills*

Good interpersonal skills are another determining factor in emotional intelligence. Emotionally intelligent people are often team players and can successfully cooperate and collaborate with others. The characteristic of empathy plays a significant role in a person's social skills. Emotionally intelligent people are better team players because of the fact that they are better able to understand and relate to those around them.

Their analytical approach makes them competent at solving and managing conflicts, therefore making them skilled at managing relationships. Since emotionally intelligent people are not egotistical, they are better at building effective and meaningful relationships instead of fixating exclusively on their own progress. Emotionally intelligent people do not merely focus on themselves. They are able to help others develop alongside themselves without feeling threatened by the successes of others. They can adapt quickly and easily and are not afraid of change. Their empathetic nature also makes them excellent communicators.

Why Is Emotional Intelligence Important?

Emotional intelligence is crucial in experiencing success in every realm of your life—personal, social and professional. Research proves that emotionally intelligent people are more prone to leading successful, healthy, and happy lives.

Since emotional intelligence provides you with the ability to identify and deal with your emotions more effectively, building your EQ will significantly improve your quality of life and decrease the amount of conflict you experience. Self-confidence and motivation are aspects that make life much easier. An increase in emotional intelligence will help you to deal with negative emotions rather than ignoring them. You'll be able to finally embrace positive emotions too. Emotional intelligence also helps with emotional regulation. It helps you to control strong emotions and subsequently avoid impulsive decisions and reactions that may come about as a result of these emotions.

Another benefit of being emotionally intelligent is that it allows you to be a better friend, parent, employee, leader, and partner. It affects the way that you manage relationships significantly. Emotional intelligence can help you to build a happier, more meaningful and more purposeful life. It affects every aspect of your life.

Emotional intelligence will also improve your decision-making skills. It will help you to avoid making rash and impulsive decisions by allowing you to deal with emotions as they occur. You will be more aware of the effect that your emotions have on your thoughts and decisions.

Emotional intelligence can be tremendously helpful to improving your coping mechanisms and your experiences. It will improve the professional, personal, and social aspects of your life and help you to manage them successfully. With emotional intelligence, you will also gain a sense of balance throughout all strands of your life.

Chapter 3: The Professional Dimensions of Emotional Intelligence

Emotional intelligence plays a significant role in the workplace. Although there is some dispute over whether or not emotional intelligence is absolutely essential for success in the workplace, it is agreed that emotional intelligence is a crucial factor in leadership. Emotional intelligence also plays a significant role in a person's influence over others. Influence, as anyone in the business world knows, is a tool that can be very handy in the corporate sector. Emotionally intelligent people are able to master the skill of persuasion, which can be put to incredible use in the professional sector. Improving your emotional intelligence will help you to better utilize persuasion through the development of empathy and social skills.

The Importance of EQ in the Workplace

Although IQ is an important quality in the workplace, emotional intelligence sets you apart from others in the corporate sector. Emotional intelligence is an especially important characteristic in leadership—and not everyone has it. Teamwork is an essential part of the working experience, which is why emotional intelligence is so important in the professional world. Studies also suggest that emotional intelligence is directly linked to performance and that emotionally intelligent people tend to perform better in general. People who are emotionally intelligent are able to work under pressure, despite the stress, more efficiently. They can also solve conflicts with ease.

Emotionally intelligent professionals also tend to respond with empathy. They are able to evaluate the effect of their emotions, reactions, and decisions on themselves and their colleagues. Before being able to improve and bring out the best in your team, one has to first be able to bring out the best in oneself. Influential leaders lead by example, and being emotionally intelligent is definitely an example you want to set. Empathy enables you to communicate more clearly than most. It significantly reduces the chances of miscommunication and misunderstanding. Emotional intelligence allows you to better support your employees and create a more positive environment. Creating a positive environment will enable your employees and colleagues to work harder and more productively, since it increases their motivation and drive. Emotional intelligence drives personal excellence and therefore creates a much better employee and leader.

Emotional intelligence may not be the only prerequisite for experiencing success in the workplace, but it does increase your chances of succeeding significantly. Emotionally intelligent people are better at identifying their own needs and the needs of others. This means that they are able to fulfil their needs and the needs of those around them, creating a positive and fulfilling working environment. Emotional intelligence has the potential to improve morale in the workplace. Emotionally intelligent people are not only good at achieving their own goals, but they can also help others achieve their potential too.

In today's modern world, communication is key. Since emotionally intelligent people are good communicators, this makes them a tremendous asset in the workplace. They are able to avoid unnecessary conflict and can solve conflicts peacefully as needed. Emotionally intelligent people are also better at determining win-win situations since they are more skilled at considering various perspectives simultaneously and empathizing with others. They are often adept at finding common ground—a skill that is definitely advantageous—if not priceless—in the workplace.

Signs of Low EQ in the Workplace

There are numerous signs of low emotional intelligence that manifest in people at work. These signs are easy to identify, and you might be surprised by the number of people you work with who exhibit them. You may even detect them in yourself.

1. Lack of responsibility

People with low emotional intelligence often play the victim and rarely take responsibility for their actions and mistakes. Rather, they tend to blame others for their shortcomings. When an issue arises at work, you can rest assured—according to them—it will never be their fault. They'll be pointing fingers in every direction, except at themselves.

2.   Lack of communication skills

Another characteristic of someone with low emotional intelligence in the workplace is poor communication skills. Communicating in the workplace isn't easy, by default, but most people can communicate what they need to communicate assertively, without upsetting coworkers. Those with a low EQ, on the other hand, often come across as passive, aggressive, or passive-aggressive.

3.   Lack of people skills

People who lack emotional intelligence often lack people skills. They tend to refuse to work in teams because they are unable to maintain healthy relationships. Getting along and general communication proves to be a challenge. Their lack of empathy and perspective leave them unable to work well with others, and they are often involved in conflicts.

4.   Highly critical

People with low emotional intelligence levels are overly critical and tend to criticize often. They are quick to point out the flaws and mistakes of others in a non-diplomatic manner. Of course, coworkers are supposed to help their colleagues improve; but, those with a low EQ will seem to simply be breaking people down. Rather than constructive criticism, they resort to shaming and guilting others.

5.   Inability to handle criticism

Ironically, these people cannot take criticism themselves. They often view criticism as an attack on their work and their person. They tend to overreact and may even resort to wallowing or self-pity. These unwarranted reactions will certainly not encourage progress within the company.

6. Inability to adapt

People with low emotional intelligence often fear change and cannot adapt easily. It might seem like the smallest of a shift to someone else, but the low EQ colleague may tend to panic when they encounter change. If they agree to adapt, they will certainly take much more time before they come around.

7. Inability to cope with failure

Along the same lines as handling criticism, people who lack emotional intelligence cannot cope with failure. They take failure personally and dwell on these failures. They tend to allow failures to get in the way of their long-term goals. They may seem to easily forget about any past successes and let the failure fill their entire view.

8. Consistent poor performance

Consistent poor performance is another trait that was observed among people with low emotional intelligence. Many of the signs mentioned earlier may be to blame for this. Their inability to cope with change, work under pressure, and their social incompetence make it difficult for them to excel.

9. Lack of leadership skills

People with low emotional intelligence tend to lack leadership skills. Since leadership skills often go hand-in-hand with social skills and tact, these people often find the job in general difficult. Leaders are expected to have people skills, take responsibility, and encourage their employees. Those with a low EQ will clearly struggle. They may not cope well with the minimal requirements of the workplace, let alone a leadership position.

10. Inability to handle stress

People who lack emotional intelligence are easily stressed and tend to be irritable. An inability to handle stress has a knock-on effect, too. Poorly managed stress makes a person hard to work with and makes the communication process significantly more difficult.

Signs of High EQ in the Workplace

People with high levels of emotional intelligence often make better leaders and tend to possess a number of leadership qualities naturally. Their empathy and social skills make them better communicators and their motivation drives them to not only improve themselves, but also to help others improve. They are more prone to introspection and are therefore better able to reflect on their failures and successes.

1. Tactful decision-making skills

People with high levels of emotional intelligence are often much more effective at decision-making and problem-solving. Their respectful and considerate nature allows them to avoid conflict and prevents them from making rash and impulsive decisions.

2. Able to work under pressure

Emotionally intelligent people are able to work well in high-stress situations and do not easily fold under pressure. They use the pressure as a motivator not a hurdle. The presence of pressure does not visibly affect their behavior or how they treat others either. They are cool and calm.

3. Conflict-management skills

In case of conflict, people with a high level of emotional intelligence are better able to solve conflicts as they are able to empathize and consider multiple perspectives. Their sophisticated decision-making skills also come in handy during times of conflict.

4. Empathetic

Empathy is one of the central characteristics of people with high levels of emotional intelligence. They are able to listen attentively and sympathize with those around them. They are also more capable of putting themselves in the other person's proverbial shoes, and are therefore able to better grasp other perspectives more easily.

5. Reflect constructively on criticism

Instead of simply reacting to criticism, people with high levels of emotional intelligence can listen, reflect, and respond to criticism in a manner that is constructive and beneficial to the workplace.

They realize that criticism can be useful and can help them to improve themselves and their performance. They are therefore able to benefit from criticism, rather than considering it an attack on their character or efforts. They use it as a tool for progress.

6.   Able to manage difficult situations

Emotionally intelligent people are able to successfully manage difficult situations, rather than avoiding or running away from these situations. They remain calm and collected and respond to these situations in a responsible and logical manner. They are able to take a step back and make smart, deliberate choices to solve the problem.

7.   Respected

Emotionally intelligent people are often respected by those around them. This is because of their empathetic nature and their efforts to understand others. Emotionally intelligent people are more likeable in general. They make coworkers want to be more like them.

8.   Acknowledges the efforts of others

People with a high level of emotional intelligence are able to put their own interests aside and take the time to praise the efforts of others. They are confident in their own work and therefore do not feel the need to constantly defend and gloat solely about themselves. They encourage and build up those around them by acknowledging others' accomplishments—big and small.

9.   Provide helpful feedback

Along with being able to take criticism constructively, emotionally intelligent people are able to offer helpful and constructive feedback. They can analyze a situation effectively and their assertive communication skills help them to communicate clearly about where improvements can be made and which aspects were effective.

Chapter 4: The Social Dimensions of Emotional Intelligence

Considering the empathetic and social nature of emotional intelligence, it plays a significant and important role in the social sector of your life. Improving your emotional intelligence will help you to create more meaningful relationships, communicate more effectively and will significantly improve your conflict-resolution skills. People with a higher level of emotional intelligence tend to have longer lasting and more meaningful relationships, and are able to avoid unnecessary conflicts.

The Importance of Emotional Intelligence in Relationships

There are a number of things that signify the importance of emotional intelligence in the social sector of your life. A lack of emotional intelligence can easily lead to unnecessary conflict, miscommunication, and misunderstanding in relationships. Since emotional intelligence helps you to consider others' perspectives and understand their emotions, it will help you to better manage your relationships. Emotional intelligence helps you to recognize what does and does not work in a relationship, enabling you to make an informed decision about all of the relationships in your life. Emotional intelligence also helps you to be more aware of changes in relationships, which helps you to evaluate these relationships along the way. Being aware of these changes might help you to avoid conflict and miscommunication at a later stage in the relationship. Having higher levels of emotional intelligence therefore provides you with better insight into your relationships, which can ensure all of your social relationships are successful.

Big emotions are natural in social relationships. Since emotional intelligence helps you to regulate and understand your emotions, being emotionally intelligent significantly reduces the risk of reacting impulsively when your emotions flare up. Impulsive reactions can be very damaging to relationships. These damages may be irreparable and can easily become the cause of countless heated conflicts and even the end of some relationships. Impulsive reactions may lead you to say something that you don't mean, that will inevitably hurt the other person. Being able to control your emotions and avoid impulsive reactions will save you (and those around you) from a significant amount of grief and discomfort.

Emotional intelligence allows for deeper connections and more meaningful relationships to be fostered through empathy. With high levels of emotional intelligence comes great responsibility, however. Being tuned in to others' emotions may give you an upper hand and can easily be used for selfish purposes. Beware of manipulating others for your own selfish interests. Manipulation is unhealthy and can be very damaging to the other person in the relationship. Manipulation should not be part of any relationship.

Signs of Low EQ in Relationships

Being in a relationship with someone who has low levels of emotional intelligence can be severely damaging and draining. Similarly, having a low level of emotional intelligence can have the same effect on those around you. It is therefore important to take note of the signs of low emotional intelligence in a relationship. This will not only help you to identify those with low levels of emotional intelligence. It will also help you to determine where you are, and how many aspects you need to work on in order to improve your emotional intelligence.

1. Tendency to argue

People with a low level of emotional intelligence are quick to argue and tend to transform even the simplest of discussions into an argument. They are insecure in themselves and therefore tend to be extremely confrontational.

2. Inability to take criticism

Since people with low levels of emotional intelligence are so insecure and defensive, they tend to take criticism very poorly. They often see criticism as an attack on their character and themselves personally.

3.   Lack of responsibility

People with a low level of intelligence tend to blame others for their mistakes. They rarely take responsibility for their actions and are quick to blame others. In a healthy relationship, both parties need to accept responsibility for nurturing it.

4.   Emotionally temperamental

People who lack emotional intelligence are prone to emotional outbursts. Since they fail to identify and acknowledge their emotions, they are unable to process these emotions. Consequently, they end up erupting much like the volcano analogy in Chapter One. Similarly, people who lack emotional intelligence also have difficulty controlling their emotions. They tend to make rash and impulsive decisions based on how they feel because they are unable to effectively identify and process their emotions.

5.   Accuse others of being oversensitive

Ironically, people with low levels of emotional intelligence tend to accuse others of being oversensitive. Their tendency to be unsympathetic and unwilling to consider other truths and perspectives make them blind to the way they might be affecting others. They see no wrong in their own actions and therefore accuse the other person of being too sensitive.

6.   Stubborn

People who lack emotional intelligence are often stubborn and refuse to listen to the perceptions and opinions of others. When they do listen, they often refuse to acknowledge or accept those opinions and perspectives that are not in line with their own views and beliefs.

7.   Inability to cope with emotionally charged situations

People who have a low level of emotional intelligence are unable to cope with highly emotional situations. Their tendencies to avoid their emotions as far as possible leave them unable to handle these situations. They are likely to feel uncomfortable and squirm under these situations. They may even flee the situation.

8.   Overly critical and judgmental

People with a low level of emotional intelligence are often critical and quick to judge. They easily jump to conclusions before considering the full story or the other person's perspective.

9. Dwell on mistakes

These people are prone to dwell on mistakes and tend to point out these mistakes during arguments and discussions. They refuse to forgive or take significantly longer to forgive.

10. Emotionally inappropriate

People who lack emotional intelligence tend to be offensive and emotionally inappropriate. Their inability to process emotions effectively make them unable to determine the right action for the occasion. As a result, these people may laugh at a funeral or during a very serious moment. Their inability to communicate clearly and assertively, combined with their lack of empathy can lead them to be very insensitive and even offensive at times.

11. Dismiss emotions

People with a low level of emotional intelligence tend to trivialize their emotions. They don't believe that working through emotions is important and may even believe that emotions only affect the weak-minded.

12. Self-absorbed

These people tend to be very egotistical and act as if the world revolves around them. Their actions are motivated by personal gain and they rarely consider how their actions will affect others.

Signs of High EQ in Relationships

People with high levels of emotional intelligence tend to foster healthier, more meaningful relationships. They are able to maintain their relationships for longer periods of time and tend to be happier in their relationships.

1. Communicate clearly

People with a high level of emotional intelligence tend to express themselves more clearly. They are able to assertively communicate their needs and are not afraid to speak up when something bothers them.

2.   Balanced

Emotionally intelligent people are also more prone to leading a healthy and balanced life. They are able to acknowledge that balance is necessary and important, and that overcommitting to any particular sector may be detrimental both to their health and to the other areas of their life.

3.   Ability to manage conflict

People with higher levels of emotional intelligence tend to be much better at managing conflict. Their empathy makes them more efficient in addressing issues and solving conflicts without the situation becoming too heated.

4.   Foster meaningful relationships

Emotionally intelligent people are able to relate more easily and effectively to other people and are therefore more likely to make, and keep, friends. Their relationships tend to last longer and be more fulfilling.

5.   Recognize others' emotions

People with higher levels of emotional intelligence are able to recognize when other people are distressed and are able to read the emotions of others. This makes them much more effective at sympathizing with others.

Chapter 5: The Personal Dimensions of Emotional Intelligence

Other than its benefits in the workplace and in relationships, emotional intelligence has a tremendous effect on the personal parts of your life and can affect your personal growth considerably. Mastering or improving emotional intelligence can improve your quality of life significantly.

The Role of Emotional Intelligence in Personal Growth

Emotional intelligence has a significant effect on personal growth. Motivation being one of the main characteristics of emotional intelligence, it can be very beneficial to your dreams and aspirations and can make life a lot more purposeful. Being motivated means setting goals and working to achieve those goals. These goals are not only applicable to the corporate world, but can also include your individual dreams and aspirations. Having dreams and aspirations are an important part of creating a healthy and happy life.

Furthermore, emotionally intelligent people tend to live more balanced lives. People who live balanced lives are generally happier and healthier, and are often able to achieve more on a wider spectrum. People who are cognizant of their emotions and better able to deal with their emotions are less likely to fall victim to mental illnesses or ailments. They also avoid the physical ailments that may accompany the suppression of emotions.

People who have higher levels of emotional intelligence are more likely to experience success in all aspects of their life. They often excel in the corporate world, are able to manage relationships more smoothly, and are more likely to succeed at whatever they set their mind to. Their drive and motivation gives them the ability to push through adversity and remain focused and determined on the task at hand. Their tendencies to be curious and passionate give them a certain zeal that can help them to improve their quality of life and increase their chances of success notably. They refuse to be set back by failure and view failure as a lesson rather than an indication to quit.

Emotionally intelligent people tend to be more analytical and are therefore more skilled in problem-solving. Problem-solving skills can be very useful and beneficial, as facing problems is an inevitability in life.

Emotional intelligence also helps with stress-management and coping under pressure. Emotionally intelligent people can handle stress effectively and are therefore able to work well under any circumstances, thus drastically increasing their chances of success. Stress and high-pressure situations affect not only your professional life, but may be part of any sector of your life. Managing stress and coping under pressure is therefore an essential skill to develop in order to ensure a healthy future.

Being emotionally intelligent also means that you are able to discern between your wants and needs. Being able to effectively fulfill your needs will inevitably lead to a happier and more fulfilling life.

Emotionally intelligent people are optimists. They tend to look for the positive things in life and are therefore not easily influenced by their circumstances. Optimists tend to be happier and more fulfilled with their lives, as they are able to make the best of any situation.

Adaptability is another benefit of being emotionally intelligent, and a significant success-factor. Emotionally intelligent people are able to adapt to any situation and are therefore rarely affected by change.

Emotionally intelligent people respect themselves and are often respected by those around them. Their empathetic nature tends to make them more likeable.

Identifying Emotions

Being able to identify your emotions is essential to improving and developing your emotional intelligence. Recognizing your emotions is the first step to taking control over your emotions, instead of allowing your emotions to control you.

Emotions often come with certain physiological cues. Practice pinpointing these physiological cues and associate them with a certain emotion. For example, take note of elevated heart rate, sweating, stomach lurches and so on. What happened when you noticed these physiological cues? How did you feel? Your body will often respond to certain emotions in the same way. You may feel an increase in body temperature when you are embarrassed for example, or an elevated heart rate when you feel afraid. Taking note of these reactions and how you feel while you experience these reactions will help you to better identify your emotions.

Emotions are also paired with psychological cues. When you feel a certain emotion, your thoughts and feelings tend to go in a certain direction. Being aware of your thoughts and when they occur can help you form associations with certain emotions, and can help you to identify these emotions more easily in the future.

The intensity and duration of emotions may also give you a clue as to the severity of the situation. Remember that your emotions communicate certain messages regarding your needs or desires. Identifying the message your emotions may be communicating to you will help you to better identify and process your emotions. When you have identified symptoms of anxiety for example, ask yourself why you are feeling anxious and how you can address the situation in future. The next time you feel anxious, you will be able to work through your anxiety at a faster pace.

Once you are able to identify your emotions, you can then determine the course of action for dealing with these emotions.

Dealing With Emotions

The next step to improving your personal growth is learning to deal with your emotions once they have been identified. Inhibiting or ignoring emotions is unhealthy and will result in impulsive reactions and behaviors at a later stage.

The first, very important thing to note is therefore not to subdue or inhibit your emotions. Emotions are an important aspect of consciousness. They occur for a reason and they should therefore be felt. Inhibiting emotions can lead to a number of problems and complications, such as depression and even psychosomatic illnesses. Not dealing with emotions can also cause tension in your body, which can be very strenuous and painful. Dealing with, and working through, your emotions effectively prevents these problems and leaves you in a much healthier state.

The first way in which to deal with your emotions is by simply talking about them. Talking about your emotions offers relief and prevents complications such as depression and psychosomatic symptoms. Talking through your emotions will help you feel better.

Another option is to write about your feelings. Keeping a journal will help you to work through your emotions and also serves as a release for your emotions. This strategy can be just as effective as talking about your emotions, although social interaction and acknowledgement may be important for some. One of the benefits of keeping a journal is that you can reflect back and determine how far you've come.

Another option would be to find an outlet for your emotions. Exercise can be very beneficial to your health and is effective in helping you release your emotions. Meditation and prayer is another option that many opt for, that can be calming and may help you to regulate your emotions more effectively. Planning an outing with friends can also help to release emotions, since being with friends is a natural relaxer for most people. There are numerous other options that can be explored such as painting, scrapbooking, and even creating a blog. Finding a hobby or an interest can help you to release unnecessary stress and work through your emotions.

Cognitive Behavioral Therapy, or CBT, is also an option to help you deal with emotions more effectively if the aforementioned strategies just aren't working for you. CBT is a type of psychotherapy that teaches you to be more cognizant of your thoughts, behaviors and emotions. It helps you to identify destructive thoughts and focuses on finding solutions to these problems. CBT focuses on interrogating the effect of emotions on your perceptions of reality. If these perceptions are inaccurate or invalid, CBT aims to uproot these perceptions and create more realistic and valid perceptions.

It is important to reflect on your emotions in order to effectively deal with them. Once you have identified your emotions, identify the stressors that trigger these emotions. Where did the emotions come from? When do you remember noticing the feeling? These questions can help you determine the cause of that particular emotion. After identifying the stressors, try to identify the needs behind these emotions. Fulfilling these needs will help you to deal more effectively with your emotions.

Chapter 6: Strategies for Improving Emotional Intelligence

There are a number of actionable strategies that can be taken to improve your emotional intelligence levels. The first step in improving your emotional intelligence would be to determine your own level of emotional intelligence. I have discussed some examples of low and high emotional intelligence in Chapters Three and Four, which you can use to identify yourself with. Furthermore, there are various emotional intelligence tests that can be taken and used for self-evaluation. On a corporate level, 360-degree feedback can be used to measure emotional intelligence in the workplace. 360-degree feedback entails an evaluation from each member of the staff, providing feedback on the performance and emotional intelligence of an employee.

Knowing your level of emotional intelligence will help you in determining the extent to which you must work on improving your emotional intelligence. These strategies have been categorized and discussed according to the five main characteristics listed in Chapter Two. By improving these five characteristics, you will gradually be improving your emotional intelligence.

1. Self-Awareness

Improving your self-awareness can significantly help with the managing of emotions. Once you are able to manage your emotions more effectively, you will inevitably make better decisions. Self-awareness will help you not to allow emotions to control the way you act and make decisions. Improving your self-awareness will help you to take control over your emotions, instead of allowing your emotions to control you. These strategies will help you to improve your self-awareness.

- Be honest with yourself

It is important to take an honest look at yourself, your emotions and your actions. Being honest with yourself is an important step to improving your emotional intelligence.

- Take responsibility

Consciously taking responsibility for your actions and decisions is important to improving your emotional intelligence. By taking responsibility, you will be able to reflect more deeply.

- Pay attention to your emotions

Making an effort to acknowledge your emotions and analyzing how they affect thoughts, behaviors, and decisions is another way to improve your self-awareness. Try to identify your emotional strengths and weaknesses.

- Remind yourself that emotions are temporary

When we experience moments of intense emotion, it is tempting to react and to make a decision in the moment. It is important, however, to remind yourself in these moments that emotions are fleeting. Don't allow short-term emotions to affect your long-term decisions.

2. Self-Regulation

Improving self-regulation involves observing how you react to your emotions. Improving your self-regulation will help you to gain control over your impulses. You will be able to think things through logically and make an objective and informed decision, rather than a quick and regrettable one. Take note of the following strategies to improve your self-regulation skills.

- Remain calm

Practice keeping your emotions under control. Before reacting, take a deep breath and consider your emotions. If the situation is emotionally charged, take a moment to step away and calm yourself down. Reacting on your emotions may be harmful rather than helpful.

- Be aware of your reactions

Examine how you react to stressful situations and evaluate the effectiveness of your reactions. You will realize that reacting impulsively is not helpful to the situation and often causes long-term damage and conflicts. Take note of these reactions and think of ways that you can react in the future that will be more helpful to the situation.

- Think things through

Before making a decision, consider your feelings and how they may affect your judgment. Consider different solutions to a problem before making a concrete decision, and weigh the different ways that you could react. Carefully evaluate the effect that each of these reactions may have on the other person or the situation. Taking a pause and thinking about your reaction or decision will spare you much grief and regret, and will help you to avoid unnecessary conflict.

- Find an outlet

Hobbies are often helpful to release stress and tension, which will help you to better manage your emotions. Start exercising, painting, or drawing. Find something that helps you release the day's stress and calms you down.

3. Motivation

Motivation can be fragile and fleeting. People often associate motivation with a spurt of enthusiasm for working or achieving something. Motivation is more than that, however. It need not be temporary, and it can help you to remain focused on your goals and purposes consistently. Motivation is a skill that can be improved through a number of strategies.

- Practice positive self-talk

Your self-image plays a significant role in the quality of your work. Practicing positive self-talk can help improve your drive and self-image, thus motivating you to work harder. Not only will you work harder, but you will likely find work more enjoyable when you are motivated.

- Foster a positive work environment

Having a positive work environment makes working a more pleasant and less daunting experience, and will therefore improve productivity and effectiveness. Having a positive work environment will also make work more enjoyable.

- Practice gratitude

Practicing gratitude and "counting your blessings" so to speak, trains the mind to look at the positive side of things and to be more optimistic. When you feel demotivated or frustrated, list the things that you are grateful for. This is likely to boost your mood, and will train your brain to be more grateful.

- Set goals

Setting goals is an important part of motivation. Long-term goals help us to keep our eyes on the prize. Write these goals down and keep them close. Whenever you are feeling demotivated, remind yourself of why you started. Setting short-term goals is also important and can help you to face the challenges of the day more eagerly. No matter how small, accomplishments offer us a sense of achievement and motivate us to work harder.

- Reflect

Reflecting on your goals and achievements can drive you to work harder and help you maintain your enthusiasm. Take time to look back and show appreciation to yourself and the work that you have done.

4. Empathy

Empathy is a muscle that can be exercised in a number of ways. Many people think that empathy is a personality trait and can therefore not be acquired or developed. Although empathy is easier for some, there is a way in which empathy can be developed, practiced, and improved. For those with less patience and people skills, this process may be difficult and can take significantly longer, but it is possible. Taking note of the following strategies can help you to improve your level of empathy significantly. Practicing your empathy skills will inevitably help you to improve your social skills also.

- Put yourself in the shoes of others

When someone comes to you with a situation or reacts a certain way, try to consider where they are coming from. Like you, people often react out of emotion without consideration for others' emotions. Recognizing and remembering the struggles that all humans face will help you to build your empathy.

- Consider alternative perspectives

Try to be more accepting of others' perspectives, regardless of whether you agree or not. Practice being open to perspectives other than your own. If you're not sure you understand their perspective, ask questions rather than dismissing the other person's views.

- Practice active listening

Listen to others with the aim of understanding, rather than replying. Engage with them and ask questions. This proves that you are interested in what others have to say. A sense of importance can help to boost others' self-worth and self-confidence.

- Consider how your actions affect others

Before acting, examine how your actions and decisions will affect others. If you are unnecessarily going to hurt someone with the way you react, then maybe a different reaction is merited. it is important to accept others' emotions and make peace with their personality.

- Take responsibility for your actions

It is important to take responsibility for your actions. If you have hurt someone, it is important to apologize directly to that person. Even if you aren't aware of the pain you've caused or the mistake you've made, it is essential you reflect and try to understand how and why your actions affected someone or something.

5. Social skills

Social skills are a characteristic that can only be practiced by interacting with people. Observe the way in which you react to other people and how you communicate. Also notice how others react to you. This will provide you with an idea of where to start. There are a number of strategies to take note of in your interaction with people. Monitoring these strategies and applying them in your interactions will help you to improve your social skills and therefore also your emotional intelligence.

- Be humble

Practice humility by offering others a place to shine. Give others an opportunity to share their views and celebrate their successes without feeling the need to turn the spotlight back to yourself.

- Communicate

It is important to be open and honest. Practice assertively communicating your wants and needs. Don't insinuate, but rather state plainly what you need or want the other person to know.

- Acknowledge the efforts and successes of others

Help others to see the value in what they do without feeling the need to defend your own accomplishments. Motivate others by acknowledging their efforts and successes.

- Take note of non-verbal cues

Non-verbal cues include all aspects of body language and facial expressions and can be a useful indicator of how the other person is feeling. Social cues are an integral part of social interaction, as they can provide important information that you may otherwise have missed. Take the time to understand beyond words.

Conclusion

Throughout the course of this book it has been made evident that emotional intelligence is beneficial to every part of your life and can improve your quality of life significantly. My hope is that you now understand the immense importance of emotional intelligence, and why you should develop or improve your emotional intelligence. Understanding what emotions are, where they come from, and how they function is an important step before attempting to understand or improve your emotional intelligence. Once these three aspects are understood, you will have a better understanding of how emotions work and why they are important.

Emotional intelligence, then, entails our ability to identify, process and manage our emotions effectively. Emotionally intelligent people possess characteristics of self-awareness, self-regulation, motivation, empathy and social skills. These are the main characteristics that are usually linked with emotional intelligence.

Understanding the role of emotional intelligence in the various sectors of your life can help you to better understand the extent of the influence that emotional intelligence can have on your life. The next step would be to implement strategies to improve your level of emotional intelligence. Once you commit to improving your emotional intelligence, you also commit to improving your life. By working on, and improving each of the five characteristics of emotional intelligence, you will be able to create a meaningful and balanced life.

Whilst reading this book, you have been informed about the various aspects of emotional intelligence and its role in the various sectors of your life. You have also been provided with some ideas on how to identify and deal with your emotions more effectively. I have provided you with signs of low emotional intelligence, and high emotional intelligence to help you position yourself on the spectrum. Finally, I have provided you with a significant number of actionable strategies for improving each of the characteristics of emotional intelligence. It is now up to you to take action.

Remember that emotional intelligence can significantly improve your relationships, your work ethic and your quality of life. By improving your emotional intelligence, you will be ensuring that you become a better friend, co-worker, partner, leader, and parent. You will increase your chances of success, and you will be ensuring a healthier, happier and more balanced life for yourself.

Emotional intelligence is the key to improving your life. Improving your emotional intelligence will equip you to excel at every level and in every area of your life. What are you waiting for?

Hey, it's Terry Lindberg,

As mentioned at the start of this book, you have an exclusive offer available to you for a short period of time.

In case you forgot to claim your 100% FREE, no strings attached ultimate mindset course by Intelligence Mastery.

Please can you make sure to do so NOW!

The reason for this is in the next coming chapters I will be discussing and referring back to parts of the course that Intelligence Mastery has created for you to improve your mindset.

It will be pivotal to have this course available at all times as when learning about self-improvement strategies, the ultimate mindset course will guide you to implement these strategies in a quick and effective manner.

In case you forgot how to claim your FREE copy of the Ultimate Mindset Course, search in your search browsers URL – free.intelligencemastery.com

Remember, before reading any further, please do this NOW as I will refer back to parts of the course throughout this book!

free.intelligencemastery.com

Expert Secrets – Cognitive Behavioral Therapy (CBT)

The Ultimate Guide Made Simple to Overcome Anger Management, Anxiety, Depression, Insomnia, Negative Thinking, Panic, Phobias, Stress, and Worry!

Terry Lindberg

Introduction

We live in a society plagued by uncertainty, doubt, and negativity - or at least that's what we're led to believe. Whether you get the news from your TV or the Internet, it's very likely that you will bump into *bad* news. In fact, it's fair to assume that 90% of all the news fed to us is of a negative nature.

If we didn't know better, it would really look like we are wired to look at the empty half of the glass. The truth is that all this negativity stems not from ourselves, but from a variety of circumstances that have slowly *drilled* these thinking patterns into our mindsets. The way we were brought up, everything in the media, our life experiences, and our fears can very easily settle in and shape thinking patterns that do not belong to our true selves. Before we know it, we end up wearing anger, anxiety, depression, and stress as if they were our second-nature skins - when, in fact, they are nothing but masks that have been forced on us.

So, what then? Are we doomed to think like this forever? To let depression, fear, and anger take over our dreams and lives?

Most certainly, no: you do not have to let depression, fear, and anger take over your dreams. Cognitive behavioral therapy (CBT) can offer a way to address this negativity before it overwhelms us. It is one of the most efficient treatments for depression. More specifically, CBT focuses on the negative thinking patterns that cloud our judgment. It teaches us how to spot and replace them with positive thought patterns. In this book, I will show you all the high-level strategies you need to know to get down to the root source of your behavior, and understand why you might be thinking and acting against your own true will.

By the end of this book, I hope you will have discovered that your mindset *is* re-programmable, and that you do not *have* to allow anxiety, stress, and depression to define you - or your future. With the information and techniques I will introduce to you in this book, you will be able to finally take control over your behavior. You will be able to shape your mindset the way it was intended to be from the very beginning: healthy, positive, and strong.

Why would you believe me?

I am a self-help author and therapist who has won numerous awards. I have dedicated more than three decades of my life to innovate the fields of psychology and self-help, while trying to improve my own life and the lives of thousands of others across the entire globe. I have worked with top CEOs, experts in their field, athletes, and regular individuals - and the results of our collaboration never ceased to appear. I want to show people that a bit of training from the right person can help them overcome bad behavioral problems using CBT. Yes, that includes you as well. You too have the power to overcome anger issues, anxiety, depression, insomnia, negative thinking, panic, phobias, stress, and worries. The power to change lies within *you*.

Once you learn how to use the power of CBT, you will be able to overcome most of your behavioral difficulties by using this approach. You will be able to manage your issues better, you will be able to take control over what you think and what you do as a result, and you will be able to reshape your mindset and your life in the light of your true self.

People have paid hundreds of times the price of this book to learn the same techniques and assimilate the same information I will be sharing with you throughout this guide. I will teach you how to understand CBT at an advanced level so that you can reap all the benefits of this therapeutic approach and overcome any kind of emotional or behavioral problems you might have.

Using my expertise, you will grow to be equipped with the most important skills and knowledge you need to be able to overcome emotional distress and all the problems life might throw at you. Cognitive behavioral therapy is an incredibly powerful tool and I promise that it *will* change your life in ways you might not even expect it to.

I cannot promise you this change will happen overnight. Your behavior is the result of years and years of internal battles and external influences, so you cannot expect all the negativity to go away at the snap of your fingers. What you *can* expect and what I *can* promise, however, is that all the techniques I will present in this book are not only efficient, but also easy to implement. I will not ask of you to move mountains but I will ask that you make small steps towards making yourself *better*. Believe me, the biggest changes happen precisely when we acknowledge the power that lies in small, consequential, and regular actions.

You deserve to love yourself and your life. You deserve to be happy, to live the fearless life you have always envisioned for yourself, to love and be loved, to be at peace with yourself and where you come from. In order to do that, however, you will first have to do some "work" on yourself – and cognitive behavioral therapy will help with that.

The time is *now*. Do not postpone this any longer. Every minute spent not working on your behavior is a minute of success and happiness you are just wasting away. Yes, stepping out of the familiar patterns of negativity might be difficult, but making the change is more than worth it.

Take the plunge and dive into cognitive behavioral therapy today. I promise it will be an eye-opening experience that will shape your life for years to come, and help you build on the person you have always wanted to be. Taking a bit of time to understand the concepts and techniques you can use to manage your emotions correctly using CBT is the best investment you can make in your future.

Cognitive behavioral therapy is not rocket science in any way. It's easy to understand and the tactics and exercises I will present to you in this book are easy to follow through (and quite easy to stick with as well). What you need to do is take action: read this book, implement the advice in it, and stick to your plan. Positive change will soon flourish in your mindset and it will reflect on your person in every way you can imagine.

The time is now. YOU have the power to shape your mind and achieve the self-love, and the beautiful life you always wanted.

The future starts here. Postpone it no longer!

Chapter 1: Understanding CBT

Cognitive behavioral therapy is a type of therapy that focuses on both challenging and changing mental patterns that are unhealthy, unhelpful, or downright harmful for the patient.

In essence, CBT is all about identifying the negative thought patterns that hurt you and interfere with your efforts to *be better.*

The Core Beliefs

There are three main core beliefs that support the cognitive behavioral therapy theory, namely:

- Most psychological problems are based, at least partially, on negative and unhelpful ways of thinking
- Most mental health issues can be traced back to learned patterns in such negative thinking (which translates into negative behavior as well)
- People who have mental health problems can learn better ways of handling these negative behavioral patterns to help with symptom relief and become more effective, more successful, and, in general, more at peace with who they are.

These are, of course, the very basics of cognitive behavioral therapy; there is a lot more that should be discussed when it comes to this approach in psychological therapy. I will talk about the most important beliefs, techniques, and tips connected to CBT throughout this book. To make sure we pack this book with relevant, non-redundant information, we will stop here with the explanation of the core beliefs of cognitive behavioral therapy, and pick up the discussion at different points in the book from here on.

Dysfunctional Assumptions

As the name suggests, dysfunctional assumptions are rigid rules people choose to live their lives by. Most of the time, these rules are completely unrealistic and they can damage the way you see yourself, others, and the world as a whole.

Most of the dysfunctional assumptions are expressed in an "if...,
then..." form and they are frequently overlapped with "should"
fallacies. In other words, people who make dysfunctional
assumptions are likely to believe that certain things *should* happen
based on premises that are either just partially true or completely
false.

For instance, someone may believe that "if you are a girl, you
have to wear dresses", but that is not entirely true and it starts from
the presumption that all girls have to act and look a certain way. Of
course, this is a smaller example, but the same thinking can be
extrapolated to a lot of mental health issues.

There are a couple of common themes you will recurrently see
in people who make dysfunctional assumptions, such as:

- Achievement
- Acceptance
- Control

Dysfunctional assumptions can entirely ruin the way we see life
and the world, and they can prevent us from truly attaining our
goals. When your thinking dabbles in the extremes and when you
cannot find the "grey" shades in everything, it's hard to set a goal
that is realistic and attainable – and it's even harder to follow
through with your plan.

In cognitive behavioral therapy, dysfunctional assumptions are
approached in a downward arrow pattern. To be more specific, the
therapist will help the patient narrow down the root source of their
thinking process by asking them questions until they find the
"bottom line", which is the point at which the patient cannot offer
arguments for their thinking anymore.

Once dysfunctional thoughts like these have been identified, the
patient will follow a process of understanding, assessing the
irrationality of their thought patterns, checking their
dysfunctionality, developing a reformulation, and then
implementing an action plan.

There are many types of dysfunctional assumptions, but what ties them all together is the fact that they can severely affect how we live our lives. In many ways, these assumptions are like a "filter" we apply over everything. They never allow us to see things for what they truly are, nor do they allow us to *do* things as we want to do them.

You can work on your dysfunctional assumptions on your own, as long as you know you can be ruthlessly honest with yourself. However, the help of a professional therapist will always be more than welcomed, as they will help you truly get down to the root of your issues and reshape them.

Negative Automatic Thoughts (NAT)

Aside from the core beliefs and dysfunctional assumptions, a large part of the cognitive behavioral therapy theory relies on a concept called "negative automatic thoughts" (also referred to as NAT).

These thoughts are a form of dysfunctional thinking CBT therapists frequently deal with, and they are most commonly associated with social anxiety. However, this is not always the case, so there might be people with no social anxiety or low social anxiety who still resort to using negative automatic thoughts on a recurrent basis.

Negative automatic thoughts are very often directed at the person thinking them, and they can affect their self-confidence to a point where they fail to succeed at most goals they engage in working on.

For instance, if you think "I'm stupid" or "I'm never going to make it through this", it will influence how you deliver what you are aiming to do (e.g., a presentation at work). It will also affect how you act around people. You will set yourself up for failure by thinking you are not good enough or that people will think you are not good enough. In fact, people only see what you project out into the world. When a negative automatic thought has taken over this process, they might see a lack of self-confidence and awkwardness, but never what you *assume* they see.

The Aims of CBT

It's important that you recognize cognitive behavioral therapy is not any kind of magic trick. Nothing is. No type of therapy or therapeutic approach can ever make you "good" overnight - and, without a doubt, nothing can make you "good" if you don't put a little bit of effort into it.

The main aim of CBT is to help you become aware of negative thinking patterns: how they were formed, how you can replace them with positive ones, and how you can avoid letting them crawl back into your life again.

Studies show cognitive behavioral therapy is more effective than other approaches across a pretty wide range of mental health issues, including (but not limited to) personality disorders, anxiety, depression, bulimia, and addiction (Hofmann et al., 2012). It might not show the same level of effectiveness in all situations, but it most certainly *does* work in the vast majority of cases.

CBT does not aim to magically make you feel better. It aims to help you find the tools you need to make *yourself* better, which is precisely why it is such an effective method. In this approach, healing comes from the inside and it uses your own natural "tools" against the toxicity that has been building up in your mindset.

Techniques and Method Used

The core of the ensemble of techniques and methods used in CBT relies on tracking dysfunctional assumptions/thoughts by using a form. Sometimes referred to as a "worksheet", this form will ask you to fill in moments, emotions, and thoughts associated with those happenings. The purpose of this worksheet is to allow you to track your negative thoughts and help you remodel them into something positive.

Other methods and techniques used in cognitive behavioral therapy to help patients find the root source of their problems and tackle it in a healthy and effective way include:
- Prompt-based journaling
- Discussions with a therapist
- Graded exposure (performed with a therapist)
- Activity scheduling
- Successive approximation
- Playing the "scenario" until the end

All in all, CBT is a therapeutic approach that focuses on changing your patterns of thinking and helping you redirect your energy and your personal resources into building a better version of yourself. Unlike in other therapeutic approaches, cognitive behavioral therapy places you and how you work with your own person at the center of the entire process, giving you freedom to remodel yourself as you truly want. The reason so many therapists and patients lean towards CBT (at least partially) is connected to the special attention given to each person and what happens inside of them, rather than simply inoculating ideas and behaviors from the exterior.

Chapter 2: Understanding and Identifying Issues that Arise in Everyday Life

Cognitive behavioral therapy is used in a very wide range of situations to treat many types of mental health issues. Since one of the core beliefs of CBT consists of the idea that most mental health problems stem from thinking patterns coming from the "inside" of the patient, it is easy to see how this therapeutic approach can be adapted to suit a large array of needs.

For example, this is how CBT will help in the following situations:

- **Anger management.** Since anger management problems are usually connected to a more or less conscious frustration the patient has, CBT can help them define that problem and eliminate it in order to reshape their behavior according to the "rules" of anger management.
- **Anxiety.** Although fear is completely normal, anxiety takes it to the next level by almost literally "freezing" a person's life. Most times, anxiety is related to the less conscious parts of our brain and how we perceive ourselves and the world. As such, cognitive behavioral therapy can help patients by directing them to the real root of their fear and helping them deal with it upfront and personal.
- **Depression.** We don't know exactly why depression exists or even how it crawls into our life. One thing is for certain: CBT can help patients determine the cause of their deep sadness and despair and re-route their thoughts on a more positive path. This helps them *manage* depression in a healthy and constructive way.
- **Insomnia.** Insomnia often has a very mental root cause, but patients are not fully aware of what that might be. In such situations, cognitive behavioral therapy can help them determine what the actual source of their sleeplessness is, as well as address it accordingly.

- **Negative thinking.** Contrary to the popular belief, people who see the glass half empty are not necessarily more realistic. On the contrary, actually: they live by extreme rules and extremist thinking and this tends to cloud their judgment, not allowing them to see, ponder, and deal with life situations at their real value. CBT can help these patients rewire their thought patterns to be more in tune with reality and more positive in general.
- **Obsessive-compulsive disorder.** OCD, as it is very often referred to, is a deep fear of disorder and chaos. Most times, it is solely a mechanism by which the brain tries to set one's life in order in an extreme way, rather than a balanced one. CBT can help OCD patients find the source of their thinking and, eventually, find the balance they need so much.
- **Panic attacks.** Just like anxiety, panic attacks feel as if they come from thin air - but what most people don't know is that there is a root cause for pretty much every mental health issue, including panic attacks. Cognitive behavioral therapy helps these patients find their answers and rewire their thinking to overcome panic attacks in a healthier and more efficient way.
- **Phobias.** Irrational down to the very core, phobias are a type of extreme fear geared at very specific triggers. In these situations, CBT can help patients reprogram the way they think and feel about the source of their fears. This is usually done by a therapist who gradually exposes the patient to the source of their fear to show them there is nothing to be really afraid of.
- **Stress and worry.** Although not recognized as an actual mental health issue per se, stress and worries can have a tremendous impact on one's mental and physical health. Cognitive behavioral therapy can help people build coping mechanisms they can rely on when the stress of their lives

becomes too much to handle, enabling them to control these situations as much as possible.

Everybody has problems. Our daily lives are filled with stepping stones and bumps in the road such as traumatic or sad moments and negative situations or emotions. The key lies not in avoiding these situations entirely, because nobody can, but in learning how to manage them and cope with them when they arise.

This is precisely where cognitive behavioral therapy becomes helpful. By helping people dig deep into their thought patterns, CBT provides them with the weapons they need to combat problems when they appear.

Chapter 3: Taking Your Life Back: Proven CBT Techniques

If anything, cognitive behavioral therapy teaches how to take your life back from the negative thinking patterns that have been holding it hostage. As we have discussed already, CBT can be used to treat mental health issues, but it can also be used when you want to set goals and actually achieve them.

There are three main stages of becoming successful by using the CBT approach:

1. **Set a goal.** Make sure it is an attainable, realistic, and very specific one. For instance, if you want to lose weight, don't just make "weight loss" your goal. Be specific about it ("I want to lose X amount of pounds"), make sure you can measure it ("in an X number of months"), and make sure it is realistic (i.e., don't set a goal to lose, let's say, 50 pounds in one month).

2. **Evaluate your goal.** This means you have to take the time to learn where you stand right now and where you want to be. Furthermore, you should also analyze the specific steps you want to take in the direction of your goal. For instance, if we go back to the weight loss example above, you should weigh yourself now, analyze your lifestyle and habits right now, and devise a realistic plan on how you can change the things that are preventing you from losing weight.

3. **Deal with your pessimistic thoughts.** This is exactly where cognitive behavioral therapy can help you. The best way to deal with your negative thoughts is by creating a worksheet in which you jot down negative experiences, the emotions you felt when you were going through them, as well as the thoughts you associated with those moments. If you do this long enough, you will start to see some negative thinking patterns. Even more than that, you will start to really *know* them and where they stem from. As such, you will find it a

lot easier to remove these thought patterns and replace them with positive ones that focus on your success, rather than failure.

You definitely have the power to take your life back and reshape it just the way you want it to be. It doesn't happen fast, as many would promise, and it most certainly requires a good amount of effort on your end. However, cognitive behavioral therapy can be your support in this journey, and it can help you sculpt a life that truly fits your goals, dreams, and vision of a "happy future."

Chapter 4: Rewiring a New Attitude

Part of building a new life is knowing how to rewire not only your conscious thoughts, but also your actual attitude towards yourself.

How do you do that? How to rewire a new attitude to actually help yourself succeed?

Here are some basic tips to keep in mind:

Practice Gratitude

We might not be fully aware of this, but gratitude helps us build a better life for ourselves.Feeling frustrated and sending out negative vibes might seem like a circle you cannot escape, but the truth is that gratitude might just be the gate you have to open if you want more good things in your life.

When you are grateful for what you have, it is increasingly easy to attract positivity from the universe. Gratefulness teaches us that true happiness and contempt don't come from the far-reaching goals we set ourselves to, but from the *present moment* and the things we already have. When you start from a point of gratitude, you are far more likely to succeed in everything you set your mind to, precisely because you start from a point where you are already attracting good vibes.

Write Things Down

Writing is, perhaps, one of the greatest inventions of mankind. Not only did the "written letter" allow us to pass on knowledge to future generations, but it also helped us pass on emotion and knowledge to our own future selves.

Writing about what you are grateful for can have a tremendous impact on your brain and on your mentality. The simple act of laying your thoughts down on paper is bound to make you feel even more grateful about the things you do have, and even more hopeful about the things you are working towards.

Become a Positive Hero

Positive heroes are not only positive about themselves; they also spread their positivity with the world. Minute by minute, week by week, and year by year, these people change the world in so many ways they deserve a statue.

Become one of these people. Become a positive thinker that allows the good energies in the universe to envelop you and those around you.

Some of the main ways to become a positive thinker include the following:

- Surround yourself with positive people
- Constantly try to feed your positivity through meditation and mindfulness
- Always try to help others
- Always try to see the full side of the glass
- Exercise (it can positively impact your mindset)
- Try to find solace in spirituality

Of course, because everyone is different your positivity might stem from a completely different place than anything mentioned above. The key is to find those things that fuel the good in you and work on them.

CBT Treatments

Positive cognitive behavioral therapy is a branch of CBT that focuses on helping people find the positive inner voice. In general CBT centers on problem solving, whereas positive CBT focuses on building positive emotions.

These emotions are meant to become the central piece in the puzzle of one's life, at home or at work, enabling them to be more self-confident and more self-reliant.

Although CBT in general is all about the demolition of negative thought patterns, positive cognitive behavioral therapy focuses on rewiring the brain to think in a way that allows people to see the best part of everything.

One of the most recommended exercises in positive CBT is to encourage the patient to re-think their position on certain events. They are asked to reconsider events from an emotional and action-related point of view. For instance, if you are overwhelmed with tasks at work and you feel like you are loathing the idea, you will be encouraged to shift your thinking to instead be grateful that your work gives you the chance to improve your life.

Positive thinking takes a lot more practice than many people believe, but it can totally change not only your perspective on life, but how you actually *live* your life and how you attain your goals as well.

Chapter 5: Recognizing and Modifying Your Belief Systems

I will be completely honest with you: changing your entire belief system can sometimes feel like a real struggle. However, it is more than worth the effort because doing this can change your life dramatically.

There are a few steps you have to take in order to recognize and modify your belief system:

1. **Identify if your mentality is stable.** Some people have the same mentality throughout their entire life, regardless of how their mood might change. Other people will shift their mindset according to their mood. For instance, someone who is depressed might experience times when they can only see the glass half empty, but they might also experience times of "normality" when they can look at things in a clearer view.

2. **Start emphasizing the positive thoughts that you have about yourself.** Look, we all have negative ideas and negative thoughts about ourselves, other people, and our surroundings. If you keep focusing on the good things, though, you are far more likely to succeed by building your self-confidence and your capacity to overcome the bumps in your road to success.

3. **Work on a positive thought journal.** As I was saying before, writing down your thoughts can have a tremendous effect on your mental health, so try to do it as often as possible. If you are working on changing your mindset, I suggest you create a positive thought journal and make a pledge to write in it on a regular basis. You may not think this now, but every day brings something positive with it; a positive thought journal can really help you become more aware of this.

4. **Re-evaluate yourself after a few months of doing all of the above.** How are you feeling now? Are you getting closer to your goals? Don't you feel just *better* in general?

5. **Speak to an accountability partner.** Making yourself accountable in front of someone else will make you more likely to actually stick to your plan. You can do this online or in person. What is essential is to make sure you share your journey with someone in a truly raw and honest way.

6. **Try to discover where old negative thoughts came from.** Cognitive behavioral therapy can help here precisely because it will offer you powerful tools to seek the answers you are looking for. The simple worksheet all CBT therapists suggest can be a real life-changing experience because it will help you determine your negative thinking patterns. As such, it will also make it easier for you to avoid falling into their trap again.

7. **Watch yourself when you spiral into negative self-talk.** It can happen to even the most positive people in the world, so don't worry if you get there. It's normal to relapse and it's completely normal to feel down sometimes. What is important, however, is to make sure you keep yourself in check when these negative tendencies kick in and not allow them to take over you and your actions.

8. **Evaluate how much you accept negative thoughts and beliefs.** A little bit of negativity and realism is good in our life. It makes us more down to earth and more human. However, it is important for you to understand what your limits are and where you want to draw the line when it comes to the different negative thinking patterns that might "plague" your mindset.

Positive thinking doesn't happen overnight and it usually doesn't last forever. You can't "do it once" and then "have" it for the rest of your life. It's a continuous battle against your upbringing, experience, and the natural tendencies of your brain. And yet, no matter how difficult this battle might seem at first, it will soon become your second nature. If you work hard enough on this, you will soon be able to control your negative thought patterns and consistently replace them with true positivity.

Chapter 6: Dealing with Anxiety and Worry

Fear is an absolutely natural reaction. If you go far back in time to the beginnings of the human species, you will realize that fear not only helped us survive, but also evolve.

However, *too much* of anything can be harmful – and fear makes no exception. In many ways, anxiety can be defined as a type of fear that is taken to the extreme. In the worst-case scenarios, fear can render you numb and it can prevent you from truly achieving your goals.

The fight or flight response in our bodies is normal. It exists because it helps us determine if a situation is dangerous for us and act accordingly. Numerous elements come into play when this response is activated: our nervous system, our heartbeat, and our senses all come together to protect us against the danger.

Anxiety develops when our minds and our bodies cannot perceive danger correctly. The smallest things can become life-threatening in our eyes when anxiety takes over – and this is specifically why this mental health issue can be so problematic.

Structured problem solving is one of the healthiest approaches we can take when we feel anxious. By dividing the source of your fear into solvable issues, your brain is more likely to better manage anxiety responses.

In addition to structured problem solving, you can also practice exercises that help you manage your anxiety. Some of the most popular ones include the following:

- **Limiting your consumption of technology and messaging tools.** You might not realize this, but technology can make us terribly anxious. For example, in a 2018 study it was shown that social media use can increase feelings of anxiety and depression in patients (Shensa et al., 2018). The more you avoid these sources of anxiety, the better off you will be.
- **Meditation.** As one of the most widespread mindfulness practices, meditation can alleviate symptoms of anxiety. In

a study run by Harvard, it was shown that those who practice meditation find it easier to deal with stress and anxiety precisely because meditation helps them find a center of balance in their lives (Corliss, 2014).

- **Aromatherapy.** Frequently combined with meditation, aromatherapy can soothe the senses and help ease anxiety symptoms. Some of the essential oils you can try in treating anxiety include valerian, chamomile, lavender, sweet basil, and jasmine.
- **Taking hot baths or showers (aqua therapy).** There is something inherently soothing about water, which is why we always tend to want a hot bath when we feel overwhelmed by daily problems. Hot baths can help you make anxiety symptoms feel less harsh on your body and on your mind. Pamper yourself every now and again and dive deep into your bathtub under a thick layer of bubbles, oils, and salts. It can help.
- **Exercise.** You may have heard this a thousand times before, but if there is *one* reason everyone keeps telling you to exercise it's this: it works. Exercising can really change your mindset. It can help you be healthier not only physically, but mentally too. In terms of anxiety, exercising can help your body release hormones that deal with stress and anxiety and keep their symptoms in check. Exercise with regularity and you will see the effects!
- **Don't procrastinate.** It might seem the easier choice to watch another episode of your favorite show on Netflix, but the truth is that this can make you feel even more anxious in the end. Time management is extremely important when dealing with stress and anxiety, so try to remove all procrastination from your life. You will thank yourself for it!
- **CBT.** Cognitive behavioral therapy can also help you get to the root cause of your anxiety. Very frequently, our anxiety

is rooted in issues we are not even aware of, and a CBT therapist can help you find these problems, as well as solve them.

Living with anxiety can feel like a continuous war against your own thoughts, but you don't have to go through all of this alone. Millions of people out there suffer from the same symptoms as you, and many of them have learned how to deal with these symptoms. You can do it too!

Chapter 7: Dealing with Negativity in Your Life

Like it or not, we cannot live in a bubble of positivity. Although surrounding yourself with positive people and thoughts is essential when you want to succeed, it is crucial for you to recognize that negativity exists. You cannot completely banish it from your life because some bad things are still bound to happen. What you should do, however, is try to find ways to deal with this negativity.

What exactly is negativity?

Well, we cannot give you a definition of it. Everyone is different and as such, everyone will perceive negativity differently. What is important is for you to learn what makes you feel bad:

- Things, people, or happenings that make you talk lowly of yourself
- Things, people, or happenings that ruin your hopes
- Things, people, or happenings that prevent you from working on improving yourself and your life

External negativity cannot be controlled. You cannot fully control how others behave, but you can control how you feel when you come in contact with these people or situations.

On the other hand, knowing where your own negative thoughts come from is important because it will enable you to avoid them and rewire your mindset in the exact opposite direction. Some negative thoughts come from trauma, pain, or a general inclination to seeing the glass half empty. Others come from the way you were brought up. Wherever *your* negative thoughts might come from, make sure you know how to spot them and "kill" them before they blow out of proportions.

The effect of having negative thoughts is more than just a generally dark outlook on life. Negativity can impact your actual health at a physical and mental level. It can ruin you inside and out. It can steal your dreams and it can make you the shadow of who you once were.

Don't let this kind of toxicity crawl into your life. Learn how to manage it now before it is too late! Cognitive behavioral therapy can be an excellent aid in this precisely because it puts the battle between negative and positive thoughts at the center of its theory.

The worksheet, knowing how to deal with every logical fallacy and negative thought pattern, and the specific exercises applied in each of these situations can change your life, and there is no doubt about it.

CBT will do more than help you get rid of negative thoughts. It will help you stay away from them too. And, eventually, it will help you replace them with positive ones.

Chapter 8: The Emergence of Dialectical Behavioral Therapy (DBT)

Dialectical behavioral therapy (DBT) is a branch of CBT that focuses on daily emotions and thoughts. Most of the time, we are not aware of just how harmful every day's thoughts can be and just what a massive impact they can have on our lives. This is precisely where DBT comes in to help you out.

All cognitive behavioral therapies make a point out of showing you how your own thinking is materializing in your behavior. However, CBT tends to be more common in the treatment of certain mental health issues, while DBT can be practiced by someone who simply wants to take a better hold of their thought patterns and their road to success.

Dialectical behavior therapy was born in the 1980s and its initial purpose was to treat borderline personality disorder. In time, however, it became a practice that focuses on teaching patients how to live in the moment and be happy with it too.

There are four main principles used in dialectical behavioral therapy. These "modules", as they are called by specialists, are represented by sets of skills to be followed by those who want to learn how to responsibly live the moment:

- **Core mindfulness.** This is a set of skills the patient should work towards because it will help him/ her learn how to deal with the present moment with a calm and balanced approach.
- **Distress tolerance.** This is a set of skills used by people when they are facing stressful times in their lives. Unlike day to day mindfulness, this type of tolerance will allow you to actually deal with the bad things that happen in your life.
- **Interpersonal skills.** This set of skills focuses on teaching patients how to discover and reveal their needs from the relationships they have with other people.
- **Emotion regulation skills.** This set of skills works with tools that help patients manage their emotions better, both on a daily basis and in special circumstances.

In essence, dialectical behavior therapy is not that much different than "classic" cognitive behavior therapy. However, it tends to be more common for certain types of patients (such as those with personality disorders, for example).

Chapter 9: Understanding Borderline Personality Disorder (BPD)

The borderline personality disorders (BPD) is a mental health issue characterized by very poor self-image and defective relationships with those around you. Very frequently, people who suffer from BPD have a series of failed relationships behind them due to their erratic and downright self-harming behavior.

Borderline personality disorder is not to be mistaken with bipolar depression. If the latter is a matter of cycles, the first is more often related to moods and short bursts of negativity, self-harm, and aggressivity.

The main symptoms of BPD include:

- **Negative self-image.** This is more than just a lack of self-confidence and it is frequently connected to issues such as body dysmorphia and seeing yourself a lot worse than what the mirror shows.
- **Emotional insecurity.** Unstable emotions are also very widespread among people suffering from borderline personality disorder. These patients can very easily swing from a good mood to a disastrous one. This can happen in a way that is so recurrent that it will eventually affect all their relationships.
- **Taking Risks.** Risky behavior is very frequently exhibited by people with BPD. They might engage in drugs, alcohol, or unprotected sex, as well as a very wide range of other potentially harmful experiences and behaviors.
- **Eating Disorders.** Binge eating, bulimia, and anorexia tend to be common in BPD patients.

Just like depression and anxiety, the specific cause of the borderline personality disorder is not known. For all that we know, it might be connected to completely different problems in adults. Some of the more common causes that could lead to the development of this personality disorder:

- **Traumatic and negative experiences.** Whatever happened to you, you must know that it is OK to be human and to shed a tear or two. It is perfectly natural for you to not feel OK at all after a traumatic experience. What is important, however, is to not allow this mindset to really take over your life.
- **Brain chemistry.** It has been shown that the prefrontal cortex of people suffering from BPD is not as developed (Mayo Clinic, n.d.). This means that their brain is frequently not capable of managing the amygdala, which is where the impulsive behavior can stem from.
- **Family history.** This might seem surprising, but family history can play a role in whether or not someone develops BPD. Studies are not fully clear or conclusive about this, but there is a universal consensus among researchers that borderline personality disorders may be at least partially inherited.

People who suffer from BPD are usually triggered by certain elements. Some of the most common borderline personality triggers include the following:

- **Relationship triggers.** For instance, if someone with BPD is rejected, they might start displaying self-harming behavior and aggressiveness.
- **Cognitive triggers.** These triggers are often *very* well-hidden in the subconscious parts of our brain. Sometimes, someone with BPD might seem triggered by unexpected elements. In fact, however, their triggers are of a cognitive nature, and they might not be aware of the triggers at all. These types of triggers are more frequent in the BPD patients who have suffered from childhood abuse or traumatic events.

In general, managing triggers in the case of BPD patients is done by:

- Knowing what the triggers are

- Learning how to cope with these triggers by either removing them entirely (less likely) or by devising an action plan to help you manage anger and impulsiveness even when you are "attacked" by your triggers.

Cognitive behavioral therapy can also help because it will send you to the root cause of your issues and enable you to deal with it. As mentioned in the previous chapter, dialectical behavior therapy was created specifically to treat people who suffer from BPD. The main reason DBT works better in these situations is that it trains patients to be more present in the moment, which helps improve their ability to manage their emotions and impulses.

Borderline personality disorder does not have to be a life sentence. Like most other mental health issues, it can be managed and coped with. It might take work and devotion to make it work, but it can be a completely life-changing experience as well.

Chapter 10: Practicing Positive Mindfulness

Mindfulness teaches us to be present in the moment and to manage not only our thoughts and emotions, but the actions that result from them as well. There are three main ingredients of mindfulness one should be aware of:

- Observation
- Description
- Participation

These ingredients do not apply to all types of meditation, but they set up the ground rules for most forms of mindfulness. If you want to start practicing mindfulness exercises, you should also know that:

- It might look easy, but it is not *that* easy
- You have to make sure that nobody bothers you while you do it
- You can accompany it with soothing music or sounds
- You don't have to get stuck in one type of meditation if you don't like it. There are *many* other options out there.

What are the main techniques and exercises that focus on bringing mindfulness? Well, there are quite a few, but we will only list here the following:

- **Meditation (in all its forms)**
- **Guided meditation through audio recording**
- **The raisin exercise.** Eat a raisin by picking it up, smelling it, and experiencing its taste in a very slow way, as if to savor every single microsecond of your little snack.
- **Mindfulness listening.** You don't have to listen to a guided meditation recording. You can listen to someone reading, you can listen to someone singing just for you, or you might simply listen to soothing sounds.
- **The five senses exercise.** Similar to the raisin exercise, the five senses exercise encourages you to feel the moment through all your senses: sight, sound, smell, touch, and taste.

- **The three minute breath technique.** Sometimes, all we need to regain the control of the present moment is to simply breathe in and out as deeply as we can.
- **Mindful eating.** This is not an exercise per se, but a way of eating that focuses on the taste, the color, the smell of what is in your plate. When you practice mindful eating, you have to really take in all the flavors and the smell of the food. The raisin exercise is an example of mindful eating.
- **Thinking about... thinking.** This might seem odd, but it is an exercise that can train you to be very present in the moment (not to mention that it will train your brain to be smarter in general too).
- **Mindfulness techniques for anger management.** These techniques are specially devised for people who suffer from anger issues. They focus on regaining control from the anger and on rerouting your thoughts to a more positive "place".
- **Circle reflection.** Stare at a circle and reflect on it for a minute or two. Just like the other mindfulness techniques, this focuses on captivating your focus and on teaching you how to not multitask and truly *feel* the moment.

Mindfulness and CBT are quite tightly linked, especially when examined through the prism of dialectical behavior therapy. You cannot really practice cognitive behavioral therapy without at least one or two mindfulness exercises. At the same time, CBT can become more effective when you already know how to train your mind in the direction you desire.

Regardless of whether or not you will choose to engage in CBT practices, bringing mindfulness in your life is a smart choice from every point of view. Try it and I guarantee you won't regret it!

Chapter 11: Learning How to Regulate Emotions

Emotions are the natural result of something that has touched your mind or your body in a meaningful way. In general, you don't want to completely *kill* emotions; they are a big part of the unique and amazing human experience.

You do, however, want to make sure you learn how to regulate emotions, especially the negative ones.

Emotion regulation techniques can help you keep your sentiments in check, especially in those moments when they are most likely to take over. On the other hand, emotional dysregulation is a term used by many in the psychology community to describe what happens when emotions are extreme. In some circumstances, emotions can be in complete discordance with the accepted emotive response.

People who suffer from emotional dysregulation issues usually have deeper problems. Sometimes, they might not be aware of these issues. Other times, they might be aware but have not sought treatment until now.

Cognitive behavioral therapy can come to the aid of those who want to achieve emotional regulation. For instance, some of the CBT strategies and techniques to use in regulating emotions include the following:

- **Recognizing emotions.** Learning how to detect emotions as early in their build-up as possible.
- **Releasing emotions.** Learning to let go of negative emotions that only bring you bitterness and sadness.
- **Emotional positivity.** Redefining the emotion in your head and putting a positive spin to it.
- **Separating from emotions.** Accepting that your emotions do not define you, even when they feel overwhelming.

- **Emotional patience.** Learning how to not act on emotions, even when this might have been the first thing you'd have done in the past.
- **Accepting emotions.** Accepting and loving your emotions, even when they are negative.
- **Practicing the STOPP technique.** This approach stands for Stop (for a moment), Think (of where you stand), Observe (your situation), Pull Back (from the situation, to gain a clearer perspective), and Proceed (with whatever action fits the situation and is best for you and for those around you). This type of exercise is extremely helpful when it comes to anger management, but it can work well on all kinds of impulse-based behaviors (e.g., impulsive shopping).

You should never try to completely remove emotions from your life. Even when they might be painful, they are beautiful and you should definitely accept them as they are. At the same time, letting yourself fall into the trap of allowing emotions to rule your life can be quite dangerous for you because it will soon make you rationalize emotions. In turn, this will expose you to a wide range of dangers, such as remaining stuck in an abusive relationship.

CBT can provide you with a blueprint to use when you want to find the root cause of your emotions. Even more than that, it can provide you with a mindset that encourages you to take a step back from overwhelming emotions and *assess* the situation to find the best solution.

Yes, managing emotions might not be easy – but it is an absolute *must* for everyone who wants to succeed!

Chapter 12: Developing Interpersonal Effectiveness

Interpersonal effectiveness lies at the foundation of our evolution as a species. Fear kept us safe and encouraged us to settle down to be less exposed to the dangers of hunting and gathering food. However, interpersonal skills are what truly propelled humanity to the top of the food chain.

They say there is power in numbers, but for human beings being "social animals" is about so much more even than that. Interpersonal skills helped us build society as a whole, and they will help you succeed at whatever your goal may be as well.

OK, so how do you develop interpersonal skills and how are they connected to cognitive behavioral therapy?

Well, CBT can help you build and strengthen your interpersonal skills by setting goals for your interactions with other people. At a basic level, interpersonal skills translate into knowing how to attend to the relationships in your life, balance your "wants" and "shoulds," respect yourself and set healthy boundaries, and so on.

At a more advanced level, cognitive behavioral therapists suggest that you should have a goal in mind for all interactions. There are three types of goals you can set before interacting with someone:

- **Gaining your aim/objective.** This focuses on clarity and knowing what you have to do to obtain what you need.
- **Maintaining your relationship with someone.** This focuses on the importance of a relationship, how you want the other person to feel, and what you need to do in order to maintain the relationship.
- **Maintaining your self-respect.** This focuses on sticking to your own values and your truth, as well as how you want to feel after an interaction.

Some of the skills needed to attain these goals can be shaped through the help of CBT techniques. To be more specific, cognitive behavioral therapy can help you be clearer in the things you ask from others, as well as learn how to say "no" in situations you do not feel comfortable with.

What are some activities that will help you improve your interpersonal skills?

Well, some of my favorites include:

1. **Try Not to Listen.** This little game should be played in pairs. The first player should start talking for three minutes straight and the second player should make it extremely obvious that they are not listening. Then, the two will have to switch roles. At the end of the game, both of the players will share how they feel. Chances are that they will experience a lot of frustration while trying to talk to someone whose body language is clearly showing they were not listening. Take this lesson with you and learn that your body language can be extremely revealing.

2. **The Sabotage Game.** This activity is usually targeted at larger groups of more than ten people. Divide the group into multiple smaller groups and instruct each of them to find ways to sabotage the other group in an assignment. Ask them to write down their findings and put them in a bowl at the end of the brainstorming session. Then, bring the two groups together, shuffle the members, and re-group them. Ask the two new groups to write down guidelines on how to work in a group based on the "sabotage rules" they draw from the bowl. This will help everyone understand the importance of group communication and what kind of rules can help everyone have a good experience when working together.

3. **Counting the Squares.** Take an image with multiple intertwining squares (such as this one, for example: https://www.simplemost.com/no-one-internet-can-

figure-many-squares-picture/) and put it on a board or in a PowerPoint projection. Bring all the players together and ask them to count the squares in the picture, then jot down their number. Once everyone is done, ask each person what their number is and put it down on a whiteboard.

Then, ask everyone to pair up with someone else and count the squares again. Repeat the same process as before and then ask everyone to do the exact same thing in a group of four or five.

You will probably notice that the more people there are in the group, the closer they get to the correct number of squares. Discuss this with the participants in the game and talk about the importance of group synergy.

4. **Non-Verbal Instructions.** This game is really great when you need to break the ice in a group of people who might not know each other. Ask everyone to pair with the person next to them and introduce themselves to them by saying something interesting about themselves. Then, bring back the focus to the larger group and ask everyone to introduce the person who has just talked about themselves with them. However, ask them to do this without using prompts or words. This is bound to be very fun and it will definitely be a great way to warm people up to each other.

These are just some of the games that will show everyone just how important it is for us to communicate efficiently and how interpersonal skills can make or break a goal. There are, of course, some tips to keep in mind regarding effective communication as well:

- Focus on listening, rather than speaking
- Try to be empathic with the person in front of you
- Make sure what you enunciate is clear and concise
- Show the other person that you are truly ready to listen to them

- Pay attention to your non-verbal language, as well as your interlocutor's
- Don't interrupt the other person
- While the other person is talking, don't focus on what you will say next
- Rephrase what the other person has just said to show that you have understood them
- Keep your mind open and accept that sometimes, the answer to one of your requests might be "no."

Effective communication is essential in both personal and professional relationships. Work on your communication skills and you will reap a long list of benefits regardless of what your goals might be!

Chapter 13: Practicing Distress Tolerance

No therapy in the whole wide world can protect you from anything bad ever happening to you. What therapy can do, however, is help you *cope with* and *tolerate* distressful situations in a much healthier and more balanced way.

Cognitive behavioral therapy is excellent when it comes to this, precisely because it works with *your* current thoughts, patterns of thinking, and behavior. For example, some of the most popular CBT techniques to use in distress tolerance include the following:

Create Distractions

One CBT technique encourages you to create easy distractions to prevent negative thinking, and to help you cope with bad situations in a way that will not make everything worse.

For example, a person living with borderline personality disorder facing a distressful situation might be tempted to either blow it out of proportions or deal with it in a negative, self-harming way like binge drinking.

There are healthier distractions to keep you from feeding the negativity in your mind. You could, for example:

- Cook a nice meal
- Dress nice and go out
- Cuddle with a book you love
- Meditate
- Listen to music
- Watch a sports event
- Listen to the radio or a podcast
- Watch a movie
- Work out

Essentially, anything you like doing and that is not hurting yourself or others in any way can be used as a distraction during distressful times.

Self-Soothing

Same as distractions, self-soothing techniques help us ease burdens and relax the mind so that it can focus on the positive aspect of a situation that might otherwise appear to be anything but great for us.

In general, self-soothing techniques refer to stimulating your senses in a positive and relaxing way. For instance, you could take a bath with lavender oil, watch a high quality video of a stunning place, eat something comforting that you enjoy, or just listen to some soothing music.

Improving the Moment

This skill is excellent for those who are overwhelmed by emotions because it helps them avoid impulsive actions and focus on the more positive side of things. IMPROVE (Ruane, 2019) is an acronym that stands for:

- **Imagery.** Imagining a situation that is better than the one you are currently in.
- **Meaning.** Focusing what is truly important for you in life.
- **Prayer.** Either religious prayer or the use of mindfulness techniques.
- **Relaxation.** Deep breathing, stretching, or progressive muscle relaxation for the moments when everything seems to be falling apart.
- **One Thing in the Moment.** Distancing yourself from the bad moment and "attacking" every issue step by step, one at a time.
- **Vacation.** Either an actual vacation or simply taking a break from a heated discussion, for example.
- **Encouragement.** Telling yourself that everything will be OK and treating it like a realistic statement.

These actions will help you deal with stressful moments in your life and find your center of balance again without falling into negativity and self-harming behaviors.

Focusing on the Cue-Controlled Relaxation

In short, cue-controlled relaxation is a combination of deep breathing and the regular repeating of the word "relax." This is a quick technique you can use when you feel that you are running out of control or when you simply need to refocus your mindset and your thoughts.

Living in and Affirming the Moment

Sometimes, simply repeating your favorite mental mantra can do wonders. Living in and affirming the moment means taking a bad situation and re-thinking it through a positive lens. For instance, if you are experiencing distress, you can tell yourself that you have the power to move over this and that you will soon look back on this moment and see it as an achievement, not as a bad memory.

As I was mentioning it earlier in the book, down at its very core, cognitive behavioral therapy focuses on four major modules: core mindfulness, distress skills, interpersonal skills, and emotion regulation.

Dealing with each of these modules and building the necessary skills to use them to your advantage might not be easy and it might take time for you to master them. However, these "tricks" are meant to help you - and they absolutely will, as long as you practice them regularly and truly believe in their power.

Hey, it's Terry Lindberg,

Firstly thanks for completing my book this should set you up for success by putting you on the right path.

Remember, there are particular tools that you need not just to make your self-improvement journey easier, but make it more effective.

The first crucial tool you will need to make sure you have, so you do not fail, is the Ultimate Mindset Course by Intelligence Mastery.

As when starting your journey of self-improvement, the one thing that anybody who reaches success has; is a detailed plan in place.

To create a detailed plan to have a mindset shift that you'll need to set you up for success; you have to do endless amounts of research to get mental clarity, acquire new daily habits, and much more.

Sounds like hard work, right?

Well yes, it would be, but luckily for you, I have partnered up with Intelligence Mastery. Who are giving away their highly rated course that will give you all of the step-by-step process for shifting your mindset into gear seamlessly!

Best thing about this exclusive offer is it 100% FREE, no-strings-attached. Intelligence Mastery usually charge $297 for this exact same course to their customers

Make sure to search in on your browsers URL – free.intelligencemastery.com

Good luck on your journey and enjoy the course!

free.intelligencemastery.com

Conclusion

The human brain is, without doubt, the most amazing system ever created by nature. Every second of your life, your brain is helping you breathe, walk, talk, dream, and *achieve* those dreams - and this is not just random babbling, it's science.

Your brain is the control center of your body. It decides everything you ever do both consciously and unconsciously. From how you blink now, as you read these lines, to how you process all the information acquired from this book, every single thing you ever do is controlled by your brain.

You might *think* you do some things without any conscious involvement, but the truth is that things don't have to be this way. You can absolutely take control over your mind and body and make them do what you truly want them to do: chase your dreams and achieve your goals.

Cognitive behavioral therapy is an approach that can help you with that. It can help you understand what is not going well now, why you are struggling, and how to reroute all those negative thoughts and thought patterns into a more positive path. CBT can help you reprogram your entire life according to your vision.

This book has shown you some of the basic tips and techniques in cognitive behavioral therapy. From hereon, it is entirely up to you what you do with all this information. My advice is to take it, internalize it, go through the book once more if you feel the need to, and then actually apply these tips because they *work*.

Start writing down your thoughts and emotions, noticing the patterns in your mind, and working on how you can reroute them into something good for yourself and those around you.

You definitely have the power to not allow anger and anxiety take over you. You have the power to take your life back from depression. You have the power to understand and control borderline personality disorder. These mental health conditions might be incredibly tough to deal with, but since they take root in *your brain*, it is precisely *your brain* that has the power to bid them farewell and begin a new life.

Positive thinking is not just mumbo-jumbo. It is *the way* to live. When you manage to rewire your thinking and look at things through a positive perspective, you are already in control over your thoughts *and* over your actions. The CBT techniques presented in this book aim to do precisely that: help you learn how to do all this "reprogramming" work so that you can live your best life.

I truly hope you will take all these tips and implement them in your life, because I know for a fact they can turn things around in ways you never thought were possible. Believe me: I have seen it happen again and again. I have seen people taking the reigns of their lives and succeeding at whatever they put their mind to, even when, in the beginning, they thought they could never do it.

I have trust that you can do it too. Take the lead and start controlling your thoughts to manifest themselves into positive actions that help you grow. YOU have the power - so start doing it today!

If you enjoyed this book in anyway, an honest review is always appreciated!

Milton Keynes UK
Ingram Content Group UK Ltd.
UKHW022256190124
436352UK00005B/137